THE AMERICAN FLAG

The Red, White and Blue

THE AMERICAN FLAG

The Red, White and Blue

BY JON WILSON

THE CHILD'S WORLD

GRAPHIC DESIGN
Robert A. Honey, Seattle

PHOTO RESEARCH
James R. Rothaus, James R. Rothaus & Associates

ELECTRONIC PRE-PRESS PRODUCTION
Robert E. Bonaker, Graphic Design & Consulting Co.

Library of Congress Cataloging-in-Publication Data
Wilson, Jon
The American Flag : the red, white, and blue / by Jon Wilson
p. cm.
Summary: Describes the history of the American Flag, how it has
changed over the years, and how it came to be
the symbol of the United States.
ISBN 1-56766-542-X (library bound : alk. paper)

1. Flags — United States — History — Juvenile literature.
[1. Flags — United States —History.]

CR113.W68 1998   98-23110
929.9'2'0973 — dc21   CIP
                                       AC

CONTENTS

A Symbol of America   7

What Is a Flag?   8

Flags Through History   11

The Family Flag   12

One Nation Under One Flag   15

The Design for a Nation   16

The Flag Goes to Battle   19

Did You Know?   20

Tribute to Flag and Nation   23

Index & Glossary   24

The Iwo Jima Monument in Washington D. C. shows the moment the United States marines hoisted the American flag on that island during the Second World War.

For over two hundred years the American flag has flown over the United States. It flies over government buildings, at public ceremonies, at meetings, at sports events, and on special holidays. We fly the flag to remember the sacrifices people have made to create this great nation. We fly it to remember those who have died defending our nation's values of freedom, unity, peace, and liberty—the values that form America's foundation and make the nation strong. Those are the things people see when they look at the stars and stripes of our red, white, and blue American flag. America has many symbols, including the bald eagle and the Liberty Bell, but the flag is the most widely recognized symbol of the United States of America.

WHAT IS A FLAG?

A flag begins with pieces of cloth and a desire to create a banner that represents something or someone. Flags can be many different shapes, but most often they are rectangles or triangles. They can be any color of the rainbow and can include shapes, words, or pictures. The flag and its images tell a story or message about the person, country, or group the flag represents. When a flag represents a nation or country, it becomes known as the national emblem.

Right:
Many sports teams also have flags. These flags represent Italian soccer teams.

Left:
Making the American flag is complicated and requires great skill because it has 50 stars and 13 stripes.

Hulton-Deutsh Collection/Corbis

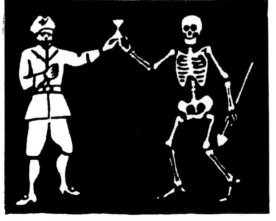

FLAGS THROUGH HISTORY

A collection of flags and symbols representing pirate activity.

Throughout history, people have used flags to signal victory, defeat, danger, and health. In battle, a plain *white flag* is a symbol of surrender—but in a car or motorcycle race, it signals the last lap! *Pirates* once flew flags with a **skull and crossbones** from the masts of their ships. The flags brought fear into the hearts of sailors around the world. Today we still use the skull and crossbones design to mean something dangerous, such as poison.

All through history, soldiers of Greece, India, Asia, Africa, and Europe have carried flags. Soldiers have always considered it a great honor to carry their nation's flag into battle. The American *military* still has **honor guards** who carry the flag for special events and ceremonies.

THE FAMILY FLAG

Some families have even had their own flags. Many such families are called **clans**. Some clans are very large. Clans sometimes use flags to identify themselves. *Family* flags tell stories just as national flags do. A clan's flag might have a symbol that stands for the family's strength, or colors that mean unity, or words that describe the family's history. The study of family history and family flags is known as **heraldry**. Some families can trace their flags back to medieval times, the times of kings, knights, and castles. Royal families, such as the family of the *Queen of England*, fly their family flag alongside their nation's flag. The royal flag describes the family's ancestry and military history.

Flags showing the coat of arms of French heraldry.

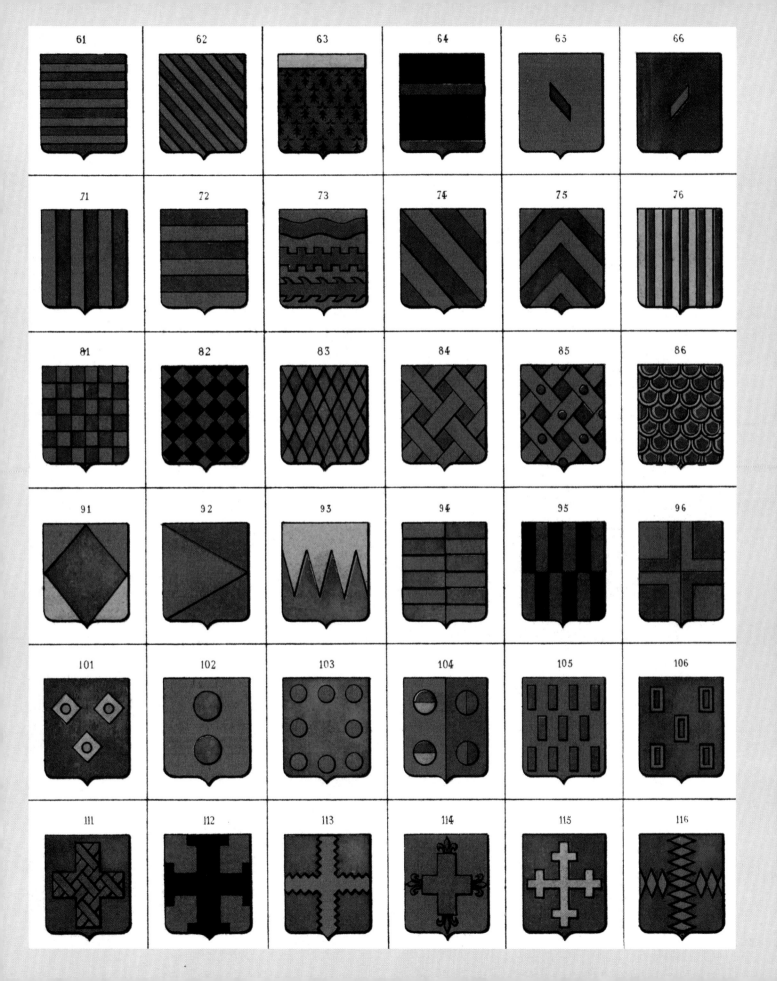

Frances Hopkinson designed the first official American flag.

Each country's unique flag tells a story and helps unite the nation's people. The American flag unites the people of the United States of America. Before America fought its **War of Independence**, each of America's 13 *colonies* had its own flag. Once the colonies declared their independence and began to fight their British rulers, they needed a new flag to represent their alliance. *Frances Hopkinson*, one of the signers of the **Declaration of Independence**, had already designed a banner for the new American navy. This flag became the official flag of the United States of America on June 14, 1777.

This first American flag showed 13 white stars on a blue background. The blue background was surrounded by 13 red and white stripes. The stars and the stripes stood for the 13 colonies that had joined to form the new nation. The stars also represented the **constellation of Lyra**, a group of stars that can be seen in the northern skies. The stars stood for harmony and unity, too. The colors chosen for the flag were symbolic as well. White represented purity and innocence, red meant strength and courage, and blue stood for justice and perseverance.

The original American flag had star for each of the first thirteen states.

Many people think *Betsy Ross* designed the first American flag, but there is no proof that she was involved at all. Betsy was definitely a part of American history, though. Her husband, John Ross, was the nephew of George Ross, a signer of the Declaration of Independence. The Ross family even sat next to George Washington's family in church. The confusion over the flag might have come from the fact that she owned an upholstery and flag-making shop in Philadelphia. Her shop most likely produced hundreds of the new American flags—but she had no part in designing or producing the first flag.

An early Currier and Ives lithograph featured an American revolutionary officer or soldier next to an American flag marked "1776."

In August of 1777, the American troops at Fort Schuyler, New York, were under heavy attack from British troops. The American soldiers, known as **patriots**, had no flag of their own. They decided to quickly make a flag they could fly above their fort. The soldiers rounded up scraps of cloth from all over the fort. They used the white shirts of their uniforms to make the white stars and stripes. They cut up their own personal clothing to make red stripes. *Captain Abraham Swartout* donated his uniform coat to make the blue background.

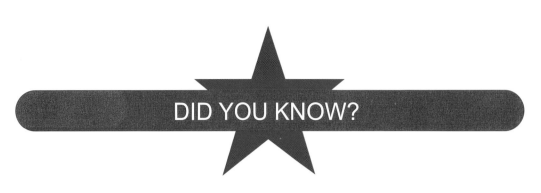

Here are some interesting facts about the American flag:

1. In 1818 Congress created a law that made the 13 stripes the symbol for the original 13 colonies. The law stated that these stripes would always be a part of the flag, but that a star would be added whenever a new state became part of the United States. The 50 stars of today's flag stand for the nation's 50 states.

2. To recognize the flag's importance, President Woodrow Wilson declared June 14th to be *National Flag Day.*

3. The flag has several different names:
   The Stars and Stripes
   Old Glory
   The Star-Spangled Banner
   The Red, White, and Blue

Francis Scott Key saw the attack on Fort McHenry in 1814 and wrote a poem about it. Set to music it became known as "The Star Spangled Banner" and was made the United States' national anthem in 1931.

At schools every morning, at sporting events, and on special celebrations and occasions, we honor America and its flag. The *national anthem* sings, "Oh say does that Star Spangled Banner yet wave, over the land of the free and the home of the brave." The *Pledge of Allegiance* states, "I pledge allegiance to the flag of the United States of America and to the Republic for which it stands, one Nation under God, indivisible, with liberty and justice for all." These lyrics speak of the true meaning of the flag and our nation. The flag is the symbol for the qualities that are the foundation of America: freedom, liberty, justice, and unity.

Displaying the American flag colors, stars, and stripes, Joseph Erdelyi, Jr. dressed up as Uncle Sam for Defenders Day at the Fort McHenry battle site in Baltimore, Maryland. September of 1979.

Glossary

clans (KLANZ)
Clans are family groups, some of them very large.
Through history, some clans have had their own flags.

constellation of Lyra (kon-sta-LAY-shun of LIE-ruh)
This group of stars, which can be seen in the northern
sky, inspired the 13 stars on the American flag.

Declaration of Independence (dek-luh-RAY-shun of
in-dee-PEN-dents)
The 13 American colonies signed the Declaration of
Independence to state that they were no longer under
British rule. Instead, they joined together to form the
United States of America.

heraldry (HAIR-uld-dree)
Heraldry is the study of family history and family flags
and other symbols. Some families can trace their flags
back to the Middle Ages.

honor guard (ON-er GARD)
American military forces train special groups of people,
called honor guards, to carry the American flag in
ceremonies.

patriots (PAY-tree-uts)
American soldiers in the War of Independence were
called patriots. Patriots flew the new American flag
when they went into battle.

skull and crossbones (SKUL AND KROS-bonz)
Pirate ships used to fly a black flag decorated with a
white skull and crossed leg bones. Today this same
symbol means danger.

War of Independence (WOR of in-dee-PEN-dents)
The 13 American colonies joined together to fight the
War of Independence and become free from British
rule. The American flag was an important symbol for
the new nation they created.

Index

Captain Abraham Swartout, 19
clans, 12
colonies, 15, 16
constellation of Lyra, 16
Declaration of Independence, 15, 16
family, 12, 16
heraldry, 12, 13
honor guard, 11
Hopkinson, Frances, 14, 15
Key, Francis Scott, 21
medieval, 12
military, 11, 12
national anthem, 23
National Flag Day, 20
patriots, 19
pirates, 10, 11
Pledge of Allegiance, 23
Queen of England, 12
Ross, Betsy, 16
skull and crossbones, 10, 11
War of Independence, 15
Washington, George, 16
white flag, 11